BATTLE
AND
ROBERTSBRIDGE
IN OLD PHOTOGRAPHS

THE AUCTIONEER'S BELL RINGS at Battle's livestock market announcing the beginning of the auction itself. The public stride purposefully towards the auctioneer's hut, past the animal pens and farming machinery (such as the early binder). Alas, the whole of this area is now under massive reconstruction.

BATTLE
AND
ROBERTSBRIDGE
IN OLD PHOTOGRAPHS

COLLECTED BY

ALAN GILLET M.A.

ALAN SUTTON
1989

Alan Sutton Publishing
Gloucester

First published 1989

British Library Cataloguing in Publication Data

Battle and Robertsbridge in old photographs.
1. East Sussex, history
I. Gillet, Alan
942.2'5

ISBN 0-86299-646-5

DEDICATION

To my two very dear children, Gemma and Kit.

Typesetting and origination by
Alan Sutton Publishing
Printed in Great Britain by
Dotesios Printers Limited

CONTENTS

STENNINGS TIMBER YARD, on Station Road, Robertsbridge, receives a new delivery of oak in the late 1930s. The four shires, all decorated with brasses, are drawing a timber tug led by Bill Barden, a local character, with his silver-bound waggoner's whip. The hand-winched derrick in the yard could revolve, with two extended legs serving as stabilizers.

INTRODUCTION

Collecting old photographs and postcards is, perhaps, one of the best ways of studying the last one hundred years of social history of any town or village. Professionally produced postcards, readily available from 1902, may reveal much of importance; personal snapshots, often inadvertently, can supply even more informative material and information about an area.

The intention of this book is to chronicle, in old photographs, a century of change in this particularly beautiful and interesting area of East Sussex. I have tried to avoid photographs of historically interesting buildings *per se*. After all, little change has taken place in the beautiful stone built medieval parish churches since the turn of the century. Similarly, Battle Abbey's architectural remains are unchanged in appearance and will therefore only feature as a suitable backcloth to other photographs.

This area is particularly rich in historical associations: Roman iron workings flourished here; Norman churches and buildings proliferate (as one might expect in the environs of Battle, the site of the rather inaptly named Battle of Hastings). There were medieval abbeys at Battle and Robertsbridge; magnificent mansions and estates; local industries (iron, gunpowder, brickmaking, tanning, brewing, gypsum mining), many alas now defunct.

Both Battle and Robertsbridge developed as market towns during the Middle Ages; a lay community flourishing immediately outside the walls of the great religious houses. The dissolution of the monasteries by Henry VIII must have caused anxiety locally but, in fact, Battle's Abbey was already in decline and only 16 monks were still in residence when, in 1539, Sir Anthony Browne, the King's Master of Horse, was granted the Abbey and its lands. Most of the older buildings on the High Street date from this period and were actually constructed with masonry and beams taken from the demolished sections of the Abbey.

The coming of the turnpike roads to the area in the late eighteenth/early nineteenth centuries was a major factor in changing some of its rural isolation, by improving lines of communication and therefore encouraging the development of local trade and industry; but this was achieved not without some local opposition. There is a tradition, for instance, that one of Battle's toll gates went onto the annual bonfire! The 1830s was an eventful time. Since the Napoleonic Wars there had been a national depression in agriculture and considerable hardship was experienced by local farm-labourers, many having to rely on poor relief for subsistence. In 1830 William Cobbett, the famous writer and radical, addressed a large audience at The George in Battle on this issue. Passions were so aroused that during the following weeks an overseer at Brede (the man responsible for administering the local poor relief) was assaulted and publically humiliated by being paraded around the parish in a dung-cart, and a hay barn at Course Barn Farm, on the Battle Abbey estate, was burnt down. Two Battle labourers were convicted of arson; one, named Bushby, was hanged at Lewes but the other, Goodwin, 'turned King's evidence' and tried to implicate Cobbett for stirring up the riots. He received a lighter sentence and was transported.

The coming of the railways in the 1850s allowed increased mobility and trade. Railway stations became important status symbols for villages and smaller branch lines sprang up. Since the 1950s, however, these branch lines (and sometimes village stations) have dwindled and died.

More recently the advent of the motor car has forever destroyed the rural serenity of much of this area, with main roads cutting through communities, sometimes destroying any sense of a village identity by indirectly causing the closure of small post offices and local general stores. Larger villages like Robertsbridge have long suffered from the sheer volume of traffic – hopefully a problem soon to be alleviated when the by-pass is completed.

Even the large manor houses – for so long of central importance within a rural community as the seat of the lord of the manor – have seen their traditional role cease. Many, like Normanhurst Court, have disappeared without trace; while others like Ashburnham Place have had to adjust to new roles within society. The large estates, like Battle Abbey or the Burchell Estate at Robertsbridge, were divided up into small plots and sold off during the 1920s. Few villages remain as they were.

The industrialization of the area had begun with the Romans and their iron 'bloomeries' and extended until the last working furnace and forge within the Wealden Iron Industry closed at Ashburnham in the 1820s. Just as the area was proud of its foundries which could produce anything from firebacks to cannon and shot for export, so Battle's gunpowder industry was, until 1876, producing the finest in Europe, according to Daniel Defoe. The brickworks at Ashburnham have more recently been closed, but mining for gypsum underneath Mountfield continues. Local traditions in leatherworking and clockmaking seem to have died out almost entirely.

This is a largely rural area: ubiquitous oast houses attest to the past importance of hop growing; now vineyards are springing up instead. Windmills and watermills were once common in the region; where they remain, like the oast houses, they have been renovated into 'highly desirable residences'. The age of horse-drawn vehicles and farm machinery is now long past. Associated trades like blacksmiths, wheelwrights, saddlers, harnessmakers and carters have all but disappeared from the countryside. Even the early mechanical giants, the steam traction engines, had a special charm of their own which is not to be found in their modern counterparts. Mechanization may have improved productivity and efficiency but, in so doing, it has destroyed much of the quality and pace of rural life.

The centuries since the dissolution have seen considerable changes in the religious habits of the neighbourhood. A revival of religious zeal swept the area in the nineteenth century, when John Wesley himself visited on several occasions and non-conformist chapels of many denominations were built — often entirely at the expense of the local congregations — throughout Battle, Robertsbridge and most of the surrounding villages. Alas, by the 1980s, chapel-going has so waned in popularity that many of these chapels have had to close their doors and have had to suffer the indignity of being sold off as homes or shops. Not all religious interest has waned, however: Battle's Baptist community remains enthusiastic while the Ashburnham Christian Trust, a more modern religious community, has flourished.

Although the book tends to concentrate on aspects of social history, the area's geographical proximity to the English Channel has frequently placed it in the front-line of England's military defences. It was, after all, one of the first areas to be pacified by the Romans. Duke William's Norman army landed nearby and defeated the Saxons at Senlac in 1066, thus changing the whole future development of the nation. During the last two centuries troops were garrisoned here to defend the South Coast against threats of invasion from both Napoleon and Hitler; while many troops camped or trained in the area prior to being shipped abroad to the fighting. Battle, for instance, has often played host to military camps and garrisons. Local names such as Barrack Farm, Barrack Cottages and Campfield House testify to this. As military technology has improved, so the civilian population has found itself increasingly involved in the warfare as the area suffered considerably from bombing raids and doodle-bug attacks during the Second World War. Much damage was actually self-inflicted, as several windmills and other tall structures in the area were demolished to prevent German aviators using them as navigational landmarks.

I don't deny there have been many invaluable social and technological advances during the past century; but I do hope the photographs in this book supply something of a nostalgic counterbalance, recreating a rural society at a time of change, with its cattle markets, horse fairs, pubs, village schools and general stores; if possible revealing some of the undoubted beauty of this particular area before the coming of the motor car.

ALAN GILLET

Battle

BATTLE ABBEY'S BATTLEMENTED GATEWAY (built in 1338), with its octagonal turrets, forms a magnificent backcloth to this packed scene of the hunt meeting on the Green in c. 1906.

HIGH STREET festooned with flags, possibly for George V's Coronation celebrations in 1911. The unlikely inclusion of the American flag, so prominently displayed, is probably a local tribute to the US millionaire, Michael P. Grant, who was renting the Abbey at the time, apparently for its gaming rights.

BATTLE HIGH STREET C. 1910, showing H. Sewell's grocery store and off licence on the left, with Harry Welfare's barber's shop alongside. Opposite stood William Wheaton's ironmongery store.

AERIAL VIEW of Battle High Street and the Abbey, giving a clear impression of the way the rear of the buildings on both sides of the High Street have been developed, over the centuries, with courtyards and extensions.

TILLS can claim to be one of the oldest ironmongers in the country, with a recorded history back to 1680. The frontage, now considerably altered, is decorated with flags as part of George V's Silver Jubilee celebrations in 1935.

BATTLE'S POST OFFICE originally stood mid-way along the High Street. Next door can be seen the shop of D. Grant, the watchmaker, maintaining Battle's centuries-old tradition of clock making. The tall thin shape of this building suggests it was a case of in-filling between earlier, probably medieval, structures. (1908.)

THE POST OFFICE needed to expand by 1910 and was moved towards the Abbey Green, its present site. The photograph, showing the new post office nearing completion, is a personalized Christmas card sent from Battle's postmaster, J.T. Dunn, to Crowhurst's sub-postmaster, Mr West.

THIS 1903 POSTCARD shows the turfs of the Abbey Green being lifted prior to its being metalled and tarmacked. There is not a single motor vehicle in sight along the High Street.

THE EAST SUSSEX HUNT (formed in 1853) meet on the Green in 1906. (There had been an earlier hunt of the same name.) Behind can be seen the interesting combination of architectural styles on the west side of the Green, with all the adjoining houses having irregular roof heights.

BATTLE HIGH STREET during the annual November Fair at which dealers from all areas of Britain would congregate to sell their cattle. Much of the dealing was done in the High Street itself.

A PLEASURE FAIR was held on the Green on the same day (traditionally 22 November) and local schools closed down — no doubt anticipating much truancy if they remained open. Traditional fairground rides such as the 'Gallopers' were steam powered in the old days.

THORPE'S. Battle's long association with leatherworking has meant that there have been shoemakers flourishing in the neighbourhood for centuries. Thorpe's has been a shoe shop since the beginning of the nineteenth century and, by the 1850s, Thomas Thorpe had expanded his business interests to include many other shops throughout Sussex.

THE ALMONRY — never an almonry but a medieval hall house with a sixteenth-century extension — reputedly had an underground passage to the Abbey. The stucco has now been replaced by tile hanging. Both the Almonry and the Wellington Hotel opposite (recently demolished) were sold by the Abbey Estate in 1924. It had been a farmhouse with 35 acres at the time and now serves as the local Social Services office. (1905.)

THE TRIANGLE, with its much loved tree, occupied the junction at the top of the High Street until 1988 when a mini-roundabout replaced it. The horse trough was strategically placed to serve the needs of both passing horse-drawn traffic and animals visiting the market site. I assume the children at the gateway are pupils at the 'Grammar School'. Where is the traffic for the AA man to direct, I wonder?

THE TOWERS HOTEL which sat opposite the triangle at the junction of the London and Lewes roads. The building was originally the 'Grammar School', a commercial boarding school for 30 boys (aged 9–16), opened in 1866 by William Lamborn. It was demolished to make way for the Fire Station.

IN THE DAYS BEFORE POLICE CARS, local taxis would be hired when long journeys were necessary. Battle's Police Superintendent James Dalmon would need to attend the Court at Hurst Green regularly, so Freddy Young's taxi, a converted Model T Ford, was co-opted for police duties. Were the headlamps painted out and oil-fired carriage lamps fitted because of the First World War's blackout regulations ?

THE POLICE STATION with the adjoining Court House was built in 1861 and has since been much modernized. PC Rodney Noakes is at the reception desk in 1966, with the cell keys on the board behind him. The internal telephone system is a fine period piece.

NORTH TRADE ROAD, the main Battle to Lewes road, was not really developed until 1920 when the Wellington Gardens estate was built on one side of the road, leaving the fields opposite to be turned into the Recreation Ground for Battle. Both photographs date from the late 1920s.

THE RECREATION GROUND, NORTH TRADE ROAD, being levelled for a football pitch to be constructed (*c.* 1930), with Wellington Gardens in the background. The mechanical digger is a Ruston Bucyrus 2-in-1 bucket excavator – probably diesel powered. The scoop would drive forward into the earth and, as it was lifted in the air, a lever would open the back door of the scoop. The unusual three-wheeled 'dobbin' cart is drawn by a tug chain.

BATTLE UNION WORKHOUSE, with capacity for 440 inmates, opened in 1834 to coincide with the New Poor Law which removed a parish's responsibility to look after its own poor. It replaced the Parish Workhouse on the site of the Senlac Hotel. Battle was responsible for 14 local parishes and it was obviously symbolic of the harsh and uncaring attitude that it should be built so far out of town. It has since become a cottage hospital and more recently a geriatric hospital. Without its ivy cladding, its bare stones look intimidating even today.

A VICTORIAN PHOTOGRAPH of St Mary the Virgin, built of stone between 1107 and 1124. It is a combination of Norman, Early English and Perpendicular styles of architecture. It contains several interesting features, including a splendid marble altar tomb for Sir Anthony Browne, several brasses and evidence of medieval wall paintings. The hand cart probably belonged to Tyrrell's.

BATTLE PARISH CHURCH has a peal of eight bells (4 founded in 1739 and the others in 1803, 1815 (2) and 1825). They were all rehung in 1890 and, more recently, in 1962, after they were sent to the Whitechapel Bell Foundry for refurbishment.

AT ROCK'S GATE can be seen the postern gate built into the precinct wall of Battle Abbey. This allowed residents of the Abbey easy access to the parish church immediately across the road.

UPPER LAKE, looking towards the church c. 1906. The row of Wealden-type houses on the left was built as part of the Abbey Estate in the late fifteenth century. Similarly the row of five cottages on the right was tied accommodation for the Estate workers. The white house on the right was where John Hammond, the last Abbot of Battle Abbey, lived after his expulsion, some of the building dating back to the twelfth century.

THE NATIONAL AND LANGTON SCHOOL was built in 1845 in Marley Lane at a cost of £800. This early print shows the building's fanciful Gothic façade. Initially the school comprised two large rooms with the headteacher's living quarters between. By 1887 it had a population of 126 boys, 118 girls and 146 infants and served as Battle's primary school until 1986.

THE BOYS OF CLASS III of Battle & Langton School in 1909. Mr Hewitt stands back left while at the other end is 'Lardy' Kemp, so called because of his well greased hair. The boy with the slate and the one directly behind were the Pantry brothers. They lived in Battle's workhouse and had their hair permanently cropped because of the danger of lice infestation. Can there really have been 48 children to a class back in 'the good old days'? So much for nostalgia!

THE HOOPYARD IN POUND FIELD, on the left of Battle Hill. The hazel (or willow) strips, in bundles beside Mr Buckman and Mr Elliott, would be soaked, interwoven and then pulled tightly, like a tourniquet, to bind barrels for storing dry materials like flour or grain. The rustic hut appears to be made of shaved poles with a roof of bark.

THESE FARMERS with their donkey cart in Lake Field are Fred Jones and George Cook. They only had two good legs between them, each having lost one in the First World War.

A MAGNIFICENT VICTORIAN STUDY of the Marley Lane junction. George Noakes, who ran the tanyard, occupied Lake House at the time. This beautiful house has now been tastelessly transformed into a Betting Office and Video Library. Much of the top end of Marley Lane has been developed since the days of orchards and fruit farms.

LOWER LAKE. Until 1924 most of the cottages and shops of Lower Lake were owned by Battle Abbey Estate. Battle's first cinema was over the stables at the rear of the Chequers but one was then purpose-built on the site of the old House of Correction, now the Auction Rooms. Mr Guy of Copps Hall can be seen with his 'chain-horse', used to help tow heavily-laden carts up the hill. (1902.)

MR STACE standing outside his general grocery store in Lower Lake (now a private dwelling). The Jubilee Tea advert on the right suggests a date of 1935.

SENLAC GARDENS, a small development of council houses, under construction in 1930. In the background can just be seen the bus garage (long ago demolished) which stood on Lower Lake.

TANYARD. There has been a tannery in Battle for centuries. In fact it is believed the monks of Battle Abbey operated a tannery and passed on their skills to the local population. The tanyard adjoined the railway bridge on Battle Hill and was demolished in 1955, when the Olivers concentrated on their printing works on Upper Lake. Battle Hill Garage now occupies the site.

LOOKING DOWN BATTLE HILL in around 1920, with the tanyard in the distance. The shed roof showing, on the right, marks where Charlie Thomas carried out his shoe repair business.

TELHAM, mid-way between Battle and Hastings, where the Norman vanguard camped prior to their march to Senlac, used to view itself as a distinct village. The nearest cottage in 'Kent View' used to be the post office until the 1920s when it became the local police house. The steamroller is presumably repairing the pitted road surface as Telham Road was not metalled until 1936. (c. 1918.)

WALTER ROFE'S GENERAL STORES AND SWEET SHOP c. 1940 originally stood in a shed across the road but the business was transferred to the newly built shop and post office in the 1930s when he bought the adjoining house. More recently it became an antique shop.

THE BLACK HORSE, originally named The Horse & Groom, was built in the late nineteenth century and replaced an earlier alehouse which operated in Hemingfold Farmhouse on the left (a building which still has its original cellars). Behind the fence stood the village pond – now filled in. (c. 1910.)

THE BLACK HORSE WINDMILL at Telham, a postmill, had ceased to function as a mill and had already lost its sails by the 1930s. It certainly made an interesting structure for a tea-room to operate in. During the Second World War it served as a Home Guard observation post. It was finally blown down in the early 1960s and now only a small amount of brickwork survives. (c. 1930.)

THE OLD MILL TEA ROOMS, TELHAM

ANOTHER VIEW OF THE BLACK HORSE C. 1920. The timber-clad tea-rooms, with its unusual mansard roof, was run by Mr Caxton and also served as the local sweet shop. Note how a space has been prepared for a fourth cottage (never actually built) to be added to the row, with the chimney-breasts already in place.

BEAUPORT PARK sits in the south-east corner of the parish. The house itself, now much extended, was built C. 1775 by General James Murray, the first Governor of Quebec, who named it after a district near Quebec. When the park was enclosed by Sir Charles Lamb, it encompassed 900 acres of land. In 1923 there was a fire, causing considerable damage. The Battle firemen inspecting the damage are H. Sinden in the helmet and M.A. Emeleus.

'BATTEL BONFIRE BOYES'. Battle has a long and proud tradition of celebrating Bonfire night which probably dates back to 1605 itself when Guy Fawkes and his fellow conspirators were captured and executed. The earliest documentary evidence, however, is to be found in the churchwarden's accounts of 1686 when 17s. 6d. was 'Expended at Gunpowder Treason' for 'Rejoycings'. There was an easy availability of gunpowder in Battle, produced locally and for sale 'over the counter'. The Bonfire Boyes therefore made vast quantities of their own fireworks, especially the Battle 'rouser', a kind of giant squib, until the Home Office banned home-made fireworks in the 1950s. There was even a fatality in Wellington Gardens when Mr Waite, a local postman, was killed when drying out gunpowder in his oven! Traditionally the bonfire has been held on the Abbey Green. However, in 1906, Sussex banned bonfires near the public highway and, until the armistice bonfire of 1919, other venues had to be found. When the Green was tarmacked in the 1930s, a ring of fire-resistant cobbles was built into the car-parking area as the site of the bonfire. During the Second World War blackout restrictions, a candle was left burning on this ring on every 5 November. Battle possesses the oldest surviving effigy of Guy Fawkes, certainly over 200 years old – after all, most 'Guys' are incinerated on the bonfire each year. Battle had traditionally burnt the torso only, retaining the pear-wood head and shoulders from year to year, until the turn of this century when a smartly dressed body was constructed – and kept! (1908)

BUILDING THE BONFIRE in 1966.

DURING THE TORCHLIGHT PROCESSION, thousands of tar-soaked torches are burnt. Battel Bonfire Boyes (Charlie Longley, Reg Wenham, George Vidler and George Prodgers) are here making some torches behind the Star Hotel in 1920, wrapping rags around the edge of a long stake before dipping it in hot tar.

MOUNT STREET was originally the main Battle to London road, with an open market place at the junction with the High Street. Many of its buildings are of seventeenth-century origin. The building on the left, now 'Friday-Ad', used to be the old Blacksmith's Forge. The delivery cart stands outside Pepper's Bakery. (1914.)

ZION BAPTIST CHAPEL was built of brick in 1820 to accommodate a congregation of 400, 40 years after Battle's first Baptist church was founded. Several other non-conformist chapels were flourishing in Battle at the time: Calvinist (High Street); Unitarian (Mount Street); Wesleyan (Lower Lake); Congregational (High Street). The tile-hung cottages on the right are typical of Battle's domestic architecture. (c. 1913.)

A LITTLE FURTHER UP THE HILL we have a closer shot of Phillip's Buildings, the oldest house in Battle, converted into six cottages in 1963 and named 'Lewinscroft', with each of the individual houses being given Saxon names. The whole building is H-shaped, with the part nearest the road dating back to the fifteenth century. It has served over the centuries as a hospital, a barracks and an inn. The overhanging bow-window opposite was part of the Old Court House and is reputed to be haunted by a 'smiling lady in grey'. (1909.)

THE KING'S HEAD IN 1910. The inn of this name had originally occupied a site higher up on Caldbec Hill, where Wellington House now stands. It has lost its stucco frontage. Mr & Mrs Clarkson, the landlord and lady, are the older couple on the left.

THE MOUNT STREET WORKSHOP (recently demolished) of Davis & Sons, the coach builders, in around 1890. Here all manner of carriages and carts would have been manufactured. The advent of the motor car turned it into a body repair workshop; after all, early cars had ash frames, just like carriages.

A VIEW ACROSS LAKE MEADOW, a panorama now protected by the National Trust, looking towards Little Park Farm. The stone cottages are tied accommodation for the farm labourers. Only the costumes tell us this is a 1910 photograph.

A WINDMILL has stood on the top of Caldbec Hill for 700 years (on the spot where the Saxon army had one of its observation posts); but this particular structure only dates back to the late eighteenth century, when it was known as 'King's Mill'. It was only on its conversion to a private house in 1924 that it was painted white. Mr C. Turner stands in the foreground.

RENOVATION OF THE WINDMILL in 1968. The rebuilt cowl has been raised off the ground by a large crane as the workmen finish repair work, prior to its being replaced on top of the mill.

A VICTORIAN SNAPSHOT of the top of Caldbec Hill. The land behind the hedge on the left belonged to Barrack Farm, with Virgin's Lane – literally only a country lane – on the left. The stone cottage on the junction was the old Toll-Gate house. The entrance to Uckham Lane on the right looked little more than a farm track.

THIS 1938 POSTCARD of Whatlington Road shows the post office and general store. It has since reverted to a private dwelling known as 'Virgin's Croft'.

PUNCH BOWL FARM, on Whatlington Road, was obviously a regular site for Girl Guides' Camps in the late 1930s for a postcard to have been produced. The house on the right is Petley Cottage.

MUCH OF THIS STRETCH OF WHATLINGTON ROAD had been developed by the 1930s. This view is looking towards the brow of Caldbec Hill.

A MAJOR FIRE caused extensive damage to the historic Great Hall on 31 January 1931. The girls and staff of Battle Abbey School were quickly evacuated to the safety of the gym before a messenger girl was sent to the police station to ring the fire alarm bell. She only stopped once, to bang on the High Street door of Herbert Newbery, the CEO, who actually arrived before his crew of firemen. The fire was spotted at 4.30 a.m. on the Saturday and, despite the assistance of both the Hastings and Bexhill brigades, it was not until 1 p.m. on the Tuesday that the fire had burnt itself out and the Battle Brigade could stand down.

AS FIREMEN CONTINUE TO DAMP DOWN the smouldering remains of the Great Hall, curious spectators come to inspect the scene of desolation. It was always assumed the fire began in the thick wooden beams built into the chimney directly alongside the empty window with all the scorch marks above it. The fireman, hands on hips, is H. 'Kruger' Crouch and the policeman to the left is PC Wally.

Top, right.
THE MAJOR STRUCTURAL DAMAGE caused by the blaze was the complete collapse of the roof of the Abbot's Hall. It is clear that the main blaze was at the higher level of the building since the massive oak roofing beams are badly burned, while the ground-floor panelling of the room shows only slight charring.

Bottom, right.
BATTLE FIRE BRIGADE pose proudly alongside their Dennis engine, in c. 1939, outside the undertakers. Since the turn of the century, Jempsons yard had housed the fire-tender, while the horses which drew it were kept in stables (now demolished) at the foot of Battle Hill – a mile away. Later the tender was hitched by tow-bar to Wren's coal lorry – with its maximum speed of only 12 mph.

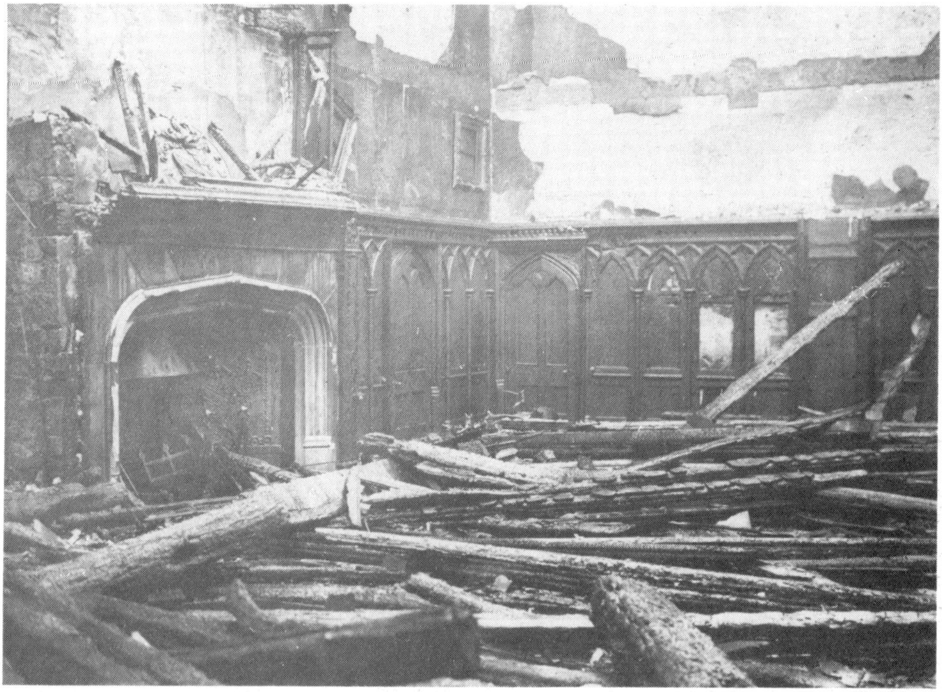

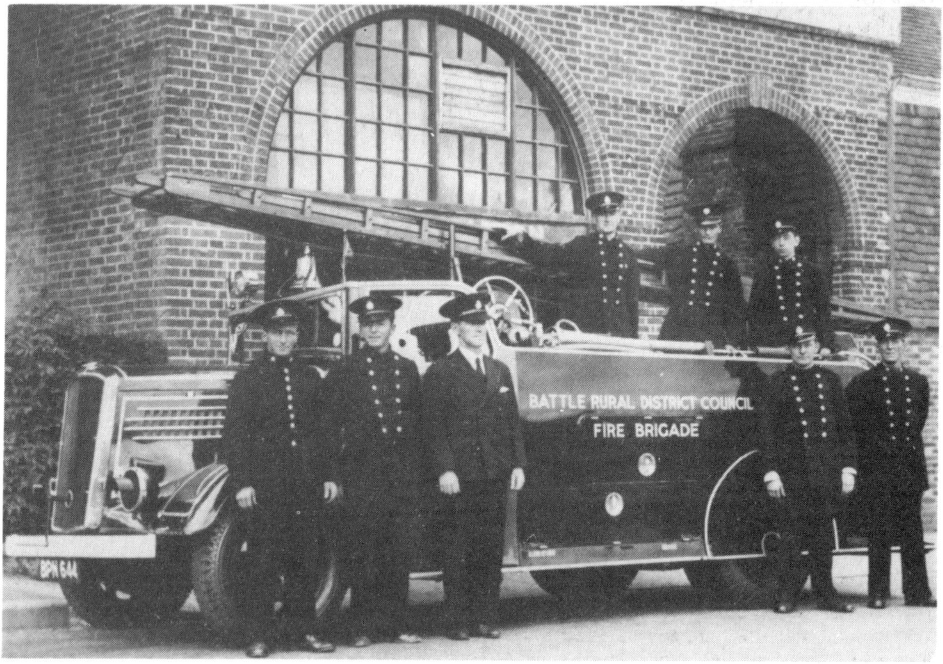

BATTLE RURAL DISTRICT COUNCIL
FIRE BRIGADE

Battle Abbey. Domestic Science Students.

BATTLE ABBEY GIRLS SCHOOL moved into the Abbot's House in 1922. In those days of domestic servants, I doubt if many of the students felt the need to concentrate on their cookery lessons! The galvanized tub on the right was a washing machine, powered by a hand-operated 'bodger' (like a three-legged stool with a long handle through it).

JACK CUTBUSH, with his double-barrelled shotgun. He lived in Lower Lake and was so proud of having been gamekeeper to the Duke of Cleveland on the Battle Abbey Estate for over 50 years that he would never openly admit to working for a mere American millionaire when Michael Grace rented the Abbey.

A DISPLAY OF TRADITIONAL MAYPOLE DANCING during a May Day fête inside the Abbey grounds in around 1908.

THE SMALL STATUE OF PETER PAN was presented to the people of Battle as a drinking fountain by Mr Thomas Lambert of Telham Court. However, he took exception to the way the local children committed indignities upon it and had it removed to the safety of Telham Court. The figure of Peter Pan is now to be found in the back garden of the headmaster's house at Glengorse School.

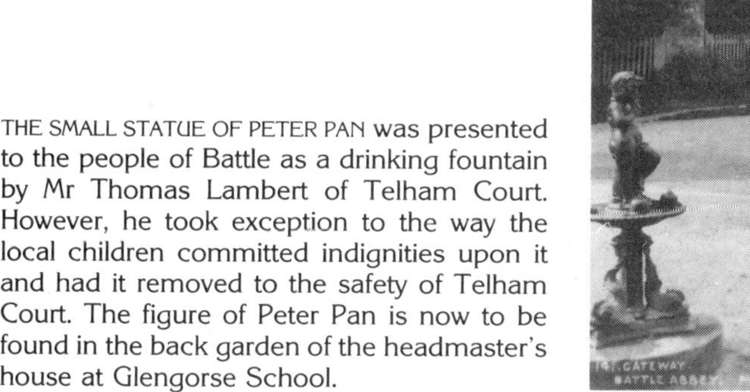

BATTLE RAILWAY STATION, taken from the bridge at Battle Hill in c. 1908. The London–Hastings line, originally operated by the SER and later the SE & CR, came through Battle in 1851/2. Although we tend to think of the railway navvies as being Irish, only 4 of the 229 men who built this line were – most coming from the Midlands and East Anglia. The station itself, a fine example of Railway Gothic designed by William Tress, still has its baronial fireplace, traceried windows, Gothic doorway, exposed beams and mock belfry. To the left of the station can be seen the trees of the fruit farms along Marley Lane. The large building to the left was the Corn Warehouse of A. & H. Thorpe, whose shop was at 63 High Street. Its frontage was partially destroyed in a storm at around this time. It is now the Granary Auction Rooms.

BATTLE TEA-ROOMS was run by P. Paine and stood on the High Street opposite Tills. Interestingly it has reverted to its modern equivalent by recently becoming Battle's first ever Fish 'n' Chip shop. (1906.)

BATTLE WATERWORKS was opened on Powdermill Lane in 1900, the water being pumped directly from neighbouring wells and springs. Previously, Battle had received an intermittent supply of water from the waterworks at Whatlington Road. The photograph shows Mr and Mrs J. Fuller outside the original pumping station and workers' accommodation, both since demolished. (*c.* 1908.)

THE NAME OF POWDERMILL LANE perpetuates the link with Battle's gunpowder industry which, since 1676, had produced such high quality explosives that Daniel Defoe called it the best in Europe. Firstly at Peppering-Eye and then at Park Mill (now Powdermill House), gunpowder was manufactured until the Duke of Cleveland refused to renew its licence in 1874. Little physical evidence of this important local industry now survives. (1906.)

A CHURCH PARADE OF ARMY VOLUNTEERS marching to church in 1887. Apparently these troops were camped at Peppering-Eye farm so they would have marched across the Abbey grounds to reach the Green – only a small triangle of grass even then. The shop on the left is captioned 'JEFFREY, TAILOR' – and certainly the local inhabitants look very well dressed.

THE SLOUCH HATS OF THIS MILITARY BAND suggest an Imperial Yeomanry regiment, possibly only quite recently returned from Boer War service. Barton's Corn and Coal shop (what a combination!) can clearly be seen with its façade masked by large enamel adverts. (c. 1905.)

SOLDIERS MARCH ALONG THE HIGH STREET in 1906. They look dishevelled and exhausted, as if at the end of a long route march, many with kerchiefs to keep off the heat of the sun.

AN ARMY CAMP. A Bicycle Battalion form up in front of their tents, probably along Powdermill Lane. Notice their rifles attached to the bicycle frames. I doubt if their training on bicycles would have been of much use in the forthcoming trench warfare of the Great War! (1908.)

LOCAL UNITS OF THE HOME GUARD (here the Robertsbridge contingent) march past Battle Abbey Green during the Second World War.

GAS MASK DRILL became a regular feature of life for the civilian population during the Second World War. A gas chamber was set up at the Watch Oak for training which comprised of entering a gas filled room, removing the mask and then replacing it as quickly as possible. The photograph is of Battle's Post Office staff preparing to enter the gas chamber.

THREE BOMBS were dropped on Battle on 2 February 1943 by one of three raiding Messerschmidt fighter-bombers. One landed, without exploding, in the meadow at the back of the George Hotel. One landed on the High Street, destroying two shops and killing Mr and Mrs Tickner who lived in the newsagents. The third bomb 'bounced' on the Abbey Green and struck the right-hand side of the archway to the Abbey. The bomb then broke in two, with one piece entering the Abbey grounds through the small gate and the other half through the main gate, scattering its explosive contents as it did so. A Canadian sentry, on duty under the archway, was actually struck on the leg by the bomb as it shot past. He fainted! Stationed in the Abbey at this time were the Royal Canadian Engineers (later to suffer considerable losses at Dieppe). Two tons of gelignite were stored in the Gatehouse, within yards of where the unexploded bomb came to rest. Little of the town of Battle would have survived had that bomb exploded. The snapshot shows soldiers and civilians inspecting the unexploded bomb.

DETACHMENTS OF UNIFORMED LADIES (Civil Defence and WRVS) march along the High Street, testifying to the way women rallied to serve the country in whatever capacity they could, during the Second World War.

A BOYS' BRIGADE UNIT, in their distinctive pill box caps, marches along an eerily deserted High Street – Sunday morning perhaps? It was the 1936 restoration of the chemist's which stripped away the ugly stucco façade and revealed the beautiful half-timbering of this fourteenth-century building. Note the ornamental gas lamp hanging in front of the George Hotel, an eighteenth-century coaching inn. (c. 1908.)

BATTLE ABBEY PAGEANT, organized by Gwen Lally, took place inside the grounds in July 1932 but was financially unsuccessful. Part of the display involved a re-enactment of the Battle itself.

CHIEF AMONG THE IMPORTANT VISITORS to come to celebrate the 900th Anniversary of the Battle of Hastings were the Queen and Prince Philip. Here they are being escorted past St Mary's Church by Commander and Mrs Ross. (1966.)

R.B. ALLWORK'S HORSE-DRAWN DELIVERY CART. Allwork's was the major provisions shop on the High Street, occupying the current site of Webb's. A local Battle motto at the turn of the century was: 'ALLWORK DUNN TILL CHRISTMAS' incorporating the names of four of Battle's leading businessmen.

THE DELIVERY CART of Oliver's the Baker. Mrs Oliver's confectioner's shop and bakery stood on the High Street. (c. 1908.)

THE MILK CART OF MR WATT, of Park Dairy, Little Park Farm. It is rather an elaborate spindle-framed cart – not a standard Sussex design.

LOCAL HAYTRUSSERS, believed to be the Parks brothers, at work; possibly at Little Park Farm. They seem to be binding a compressed bale which has been cut from the hayrick. The lifting tackle is made of pulleys and a counter-balancing weight, supported on shear-legs. (c. 1910.)

HENRY NEWBERY began his business career in Battle in the 1840s as a baker and then extended his business to confectionery (hard boiled sweets in particular) before moving on to jam making in the factory behind the High Street. The ladies of Newbery's sort apples for pulping and canning in 1950.

NEWBERY WORKMEN sit on a converted Singer automobile used to tow a trailer within the factory area. It had a low ratio back-axle fitted to its chassis giving it a top speed of 25mph; two gears only, one forward, one reverse; and was fitted with cavalry wheels with heavy cast iron spokes. The car was scrapped in 1939 as a result of the wartime petrol shortages. (c. 1936.)

EARLIER THIS CENTURY the family also operated a tea shop on the High Street, alongside the factory entrance. The adjoining shop of T. Sheather reveals the changing transport needs of the neighbourhood: from saddle and harnessmaking to motor engineering. It was these two shops which suffered a direct hit from a German bomb on 2 February 1943, killing two.

ALF HUTCHINSON and G. Markwick pose alongside two of Newbery's delivery vehicles in the 1930s.

BATTLE FOOTBALL TEAM were runners-up in the Sedlescombe League in 1923. The team members are: J. Brackpool, C. Longley, F. Cooper, R. Jennings, F. Douch, R. Eldridge, D. Gander, S. Day, ? Mitchell, V. Wheaton, E. Elliott. The building on the left is the old Drill Hall with the police station and court house across the road on the right.

BATTLE'S CYCLE SPEEDWAY TEAM. In this popular sport of the 1950s, participants rode track bikes on either cinder or dirt tracks.

Netherfield

A GROUP OF CYCLISTS pose for a photograph on Long Reach, the wooded hill leading from the 'Squirrel' corner to Netherfield which is part of the old coach road to Heathfield. (c. 1900.)

THE WHITE HART stands in a prominent position on the Battle – Heathfield road and has been considerably extended since this photograph was taken. Its situation on the brow of the ridge gives it magnificent views to the coast. (c. 1914.)

THE NETHERFIELD ARMS was built in the late seventeenth century as an alehouse, i.e., an inn which could sell beer (probably brewed on the premises) but no spirits. (c. 1914.)

Brightling

THE VILLAGE OF BRIGHTLING spreads over a wide area, its lanes following the outer edge of Brightling Park. A cart laden with faggots negotiates the village's centre which clusters around the church and general stores/post office.

THE FULLER'S ARMS, according to legend, was built in its present position at Oxley Green in 1834 after an agreement between Jack Fuller and the local vicar. This allowed the eccentric squire the right to be buried in a pyramid tomb in the churchyard in exchange for his closing the village pub, then the Green Man, (which was too close to the church and so tempting the parishioners) and rebuilding it elsewhere.

IN THE GROUNDS OF ST THOMAS A BECKET'S, the parish church, stands the strangest of all Jack Fuller's constructions: his pyramidal tomb. When essential repair work was recently carried out, contrary to local legend, no evidence was found of the massive gentleman dressed for dinner, sitting upright before an iron table laid out with food and wine. Rather disappointingly he was buried in a more mundane way, beneath the floor of the tomb. Built in 1810, the structure was not needed as Mad Jack's mausoleum for a further 24 years.

THE GREEN MAN INN used to occupy the building on the right, which later became a general store and post office. It is now a private dwelling. The village's children pose along the street for the benefit of the photographer, c. 1905.

AS THE ROAD FROM DARWELL HOLE veers left towards Brightling, some 200 yards before the church, a lane leads to the Fuller's Arms and Robertsbridge.

HOLLINGROVE, a hamlet to the east of Brightling, in the snow. The thatched cottage has long been demolished. Alongside, the Congregational Chapel was built, since converted to a private dwelling.

THE STORES AT HOLLINGROVE were operated by Mr Pankhurst. The weatherboarded building is now a private dwelling.

HOLLINGROVE HILL — a beautiful rural scene with the lane winding across the undulating countryside. The view is now marred by the aerial ropeway of the Gypsum Mines.

THIS 1908 SCENE OF THE LONGHOUSES has changed little over the past 80 years. These six cottages were originally built as accommodation for the Brightling Park Estate workers.

THE REAR OF THE ORIGINAL SAW-MILLS within Brightling Park. The old water-powered mill is seen in a very poor state of repair prior to its demolition and rebuilding. Seated is the millwright whose task would be to 'dress' the stones, i.e., rechannel the worn-out grooves on the surface of each large millstone.

A POSED PHOTOGRAPH OF ALFRED MEPHAM, clay pipe in mouth, breaking stones into small, uniformly-sized pieces, probably for filling-in purposes on the Park wall.

BIRCHEN FARMHOUSE under construction to the south of the village. Obviously safety helmets were not yet compulsory in the building industry!

THE BUILDERS of the Brightling Park Estate pose for a team photograph, each clutching a symbol of his profession: trowel, shovel, saw, hammer, paint pot and brush, axe head and even a circular saw blade.

A TEAM OF YOKED OXEN operating at Michael's Platt. Driving them is J. Pont. The goad with its pointed end was used to prod the oxen into activity since a whip was often ignored by the thick-skinned creatures. Mr Pont's dress suggests a date of 1890.

LOCAL SHEPHERD, JOSEPH MUDDLE, is holding a crook of the conventional East Sussex design. The fence behind is constructed of hazel hurdles.

A TUMBLE CART AT GLEBE FARM, led by Robert Muddle, in c. 1920. I assume the structure behind is a water storage tank with its lid held down by bricks.

THE KEEPERS AND BEATERS of Brightling Park, in a posed photograph, attest to the frequent hunting and shooting parties which would have been a regular activity within the estate's social calendar.

A TYPICAL RURAL SCENE in the wooded lanes around Brightling. On the side of the tip cart can be deciphered: T. CROFT, BUILDER, BRIGHTLING.

BRIGHTLING'S SCHOOLCHILDREN, the girls in their white pinafores, pose for the camera in the month the First World War ended. Brightling School, standing on the corner opposite the village stores, is now a private house. Mr Winchester and Miss Bates pose with their charges.

Dallington and Wood's Corner

THE OLD MANOR, built in 1380 as the local manorial court, was only returned to its original three-bay hall house design in its 1954 renovation, when the asbestos clad extension was demolished and the thatched roof replaced. Internally the house has retained an original diagonal dragon beam with unusual herring-bone beams off it. The wooden hut, now demolished, served as the village butcher's shop and was run by R.E. Noakes. (1910.)

THE STREET had a fine yew arch even in 1909. At this time the village post office was further along on the left and run by the two Miss Peters, while their brother ran the general stores clearly visible on the left.

A CLOSER STUDY OF DALLINGTON'S GENERAL STORE. By the mid-1920s the old post office had closed down and become incorporated into Henderson's Stores, which stocked almost anything as well as supplying teas. Both buildings are now completely whitewashed, with little external sign that the White House was ever a shop. (c. 1920.)

THERE IS NOW NO SHOP AT ALL on Dallington Street. Even the post office has now been transferred to the general stores on the main Heathfield – Battle road. This building dates back to the eighteenth century and has long been a general store and drapery.

MR CRAMP'S horse-drawn delivery cart on its rounds, c. 1910.

DALLINGTON WINDMILL – a smock mill nicknamed 'Old Tom Simmons' – belonged to the Ashburnham Estate and was situated in the field next to the new school (where some of the brickwork still remains). It had ceased operating by the turn of the century and was finally dismantled in 1914 to prevent German visitors from using it as a navigational landmark. Mr Peploe, the local schoolmaster, allowed all the children out of lessons to watch its demolition.

DALLINGTON'S HOME GUARD DETACHMENT stand to attention outside Henderson's General Store, c. 1940.

THIS VIEW (*c.* 1910) from Dallington's famous stone steeple shows Brookfield, with its long garden, and the quaintly named Bear House and Frog House. The roof of the old school (1854), now the village hall, can be seen, while opposite was the school's playground, built on in 1923.

PRINKLE HILL is the steep and winding lane which leads from Brooklands Hotel to the Street. The buildings on the right are the stables, coach house and gardener's cottage of Oldcastle. A doodle-bug landed in the field on the left, destroying Prinkle Farmhouse and killing the wife of Lord Wrenbury's chauffeur. Mrs White, the farmer's wife, survived, buried under rubble in the Anderson shelter.

THE SWAN INN. This old coaching inn has stood on the junction at Wood's Corner, near the site of an old turnpike gate, since 1399. Originally called The Hare and Hounds, it took its current name from the Pelham family's adoption of the swan into its family crest. Luther Cornford, the landlord, poses outside, *c.* 1906.

AN ANIMATED STUDY of the Meet of the East Sussex Hunt at Wood's Corner in c. 1922. The bearded huntsman is Sir Archetal Ashburnham. The corrugated workshop on the left was the Paintshop – run by William Buss – with a blacksmith's adjoining it (both have since been demolished). In front of the trees in the distance there now stands a petrol station.

THE WHITE HOUSE was for many years Dallington's Police House as PC Smithers lived here until the 1930s. Graylings actually dates back to 1740 and was a general store and bakery – in fact, the original oven is still *in situ* – before becoming an antique shop. Scott Burgess delivered the groceries over such a wide rural area – and so enjoyed a chat with his customers – that it was not unusual for him to be still delivering bread at midnight! (1904.)

ON THE ROAD from Wood's Corner to Brightling (*c.* 1925). The cottages on the left are now both weatherboarded and have been extended. The monkey puzzle tree has long since gone. Park Cottage now operates as kennels.

AT CARRICK'S HILL, the main road to Heathfield runs past Dallington's Methodist Chapel, the wooden 'Chapel in the Valley'. Congregations have now dwindled so much that the property is currently up for sale. Further along can be seen Glover's Cottage, where leather gloves were once made. The copse on the left is still known as Glover's Shaw.

WESTWOOD CHINCHILLA RABBITRIES (at Stream Farm). Major Simmons farmed this small rabbit-like rodent for its thick, soft silver-grey pelt. It was a noted stud farm and the public could have a guided tour to view the creatures and also the made-up fur garments. The huts have long since disappeared.

Ashburnham and Brownbread Street

ASHBURNHAM PLACE, the seat of the Ashburnham family, sits within a park of 1,000 acres, much of it landscaped by Capability Brown and still beautifully wooded. The original house was built in 1665 by John Ashburnham, Charles I's devoted friend. In the nineteenth century the façade was reconstructed with bricks from the estate's own brickyard. It is now the site of Ashburnham Christian Trust (c. 1910).

ASHBURNHAM'S BRICKYARD dates back to the seventeenth century when local brick was used in the construction of the original house. It was moved to its final site, a quarter of a mile from the Forge, in 1836 and continued to operate until 1968. The quality hand-made bricks were not made from clay but from the local sandy loam. These had to be fired for 52 hours (20,000 at a time) in one of the two brick kilns, which could produce temperatures of 1,000°.

PEENS FARM sits mid-way between Pont's Green and Penhurst, alongside the site of Ashburnham Forge, the premier ironworking in the Weald and the last to remain operating. The area around the farmhouse is full of interest to industrial archaeologists. (c. 1905.)

BY THE TIME OF THIS 1908 POSTCARD, Ashburnham's old schoolhouse had already become two houses as a new school had been built near Pont's Green. For several years, during the 1920s, the old schoolroom served as the local Sunday School.

ASHBURNHAM'S CRICKET TEAM poses in front of the scoreboard of the old pavilion, c. 1905.

CLARENCE 'FOREMAN' KEELEY, with the carter's whip, and his brother Cyril lead their team of horses from Brigden Hill Farm. The cart is laden with hawthorn and heather from Dallington Forest for bedding in the bullock yards. The distinctive split-stake fencing stood at the Three Cups Inn.

IT IS DIFFICULT TO BELIEVE such a small village could assemble so many children for the Empire Day festivities in 1909 — even accounting for the offspring of the estate workers.

LOCAL PHOTOGRAPHIC PUBLISHERS used to get to newsworthy events with amazing speed. Here an early monoplane has crash-landed at a stream (?) within Ashburnham Park in 1913 and, within hours, a postcard of the incident would have been available for sale. The photographer was not the same Luther Cornford who was landlord of the Swan Inn at Wood's Corner.

THE WATERWHEEL AND HUT used to stand in the area of the Ashburnham Estate known as the Pleasure Grounds.

THE ASH TREE INN at Brownbread Street only had its extension added in 1902. This photograph was presumably taken soon afterwards.

THE LONGHOUSES, a row of four cottages built around 300 years ago, in Ashburnham brick and for the Ashburnham Estate workers, stand next to the Ash Tree Inn. In the distance, on the right, can be seen 'Sutton's'. Johnny Sutton operated a butcher's shop here at the side of his house. (1919.)

Bodle Street Green

A PANORAMIC VIEW OF BODLE STREET from the site of the windmill. All of the Green has now been built on. The White Horse had to remove its trademark from the roof during the Second World War because it was too distinctive a landmark. When it was repainted, the horse faced the other direction.

J. BARNES & SONS,   Agricultural Engineers, Hauliers and Threshers.
Bodle Street, HERSTMONCEUX.   *Tel.* 30 *Herstmonceux.*

J. BARNES & SONS were a major firm of agricultural engineers in the area. Their forecourt is full of machinery such as finger-mowers, binders and combine harvesters. Although the firm continues to operate under its old name, the Barnes family is no longer directly involved.

J. BARNES set up his business in Bodle Street when he bought the local smithy from Mr Oxley in 1866 and became a shoeing smith. Note the penny-farthing bicycle on the far right. I am intrigued by the little boy dressed for work in his leather apron – he only looks about five years old. (*c.* 1880.)

WORKMEN SAW PLANKS on a traction-powered rack-saw bench c. 1880, built by J. Barnes. The high funnel of the steam traction engine gave a longer draught and also prevented sparks. A water cart stands in front of the engine. The building behind is the local school, built in 1860 but converted into a dwelling in 1959.

ONE OF BARNES' STEAM TRACTION ENGINES. Apparently this particular engine, sold originally to Knight's Nurseries, is still in existence at Hadlow Down.

A BEAUTIFULLY POSED VICTORIAN STUDY of threshing at Trumpet's Farm c. 1890. The threshing machine is powered by a belt running from the steam traction engine. An elevator is used to lift the straw to the top of the rick. Most farmers would hire such expensive equipment from a firm such as Barnes' whenever it was required, rather than purchasing it outright.

Catsfield and Normanhurst

CHURCH ROAD is the site of the Village Hall, built c. 1908. The small building to its right is Hermon Cottage, now used for meetings and a doctor's surgery. The houses further along were demolished for new buildings and the open land on the right is now the site of old people's bungalows. The survival of the Methodist Church, built in 1912, is currently doubtful as its congregation dwindles.

HONISETT'S STORES, situated on the now inaptly named Green, was – and remains – the only shop in the village and served as the general store and post office, *c.* 1920.

THE WHITE HART is principally a nineteenth-century building standing alongside the general store. It is quite likely it stands on the site of an earlier alehouse, the Half Moon, which was closed down in 1790 when a local weaver committed suicide after heavy gambling losses at the inn.

CATSFIELD'S POLICE HOUSE sat on The Green/Church Road junction, opposite the White Hart. It has now reverted to a private dwelling. (c. 1930.)

CATSFIELD SCHOOL was built in 1845 and further enlarged in 1912 to accommodate the increasing population of children in the village.

SKINNER'S LANE leads from the Green to the Marlpits. The row of weatherboarded houses was built by Earl Brassey to accommodate farm labourers of the Normanhurst Estate. This section of the lane is now solidly built up along both sides.

CATSFIELD STREAM is the hamlet of ribbon development between Catsfield and Ninfield. Osborne House was built at the turn of the century by Mr Adams when he retired as landlord of the King's Arms at Ninfield. (1908.)

TOM SHEATHER originally set up his workshop as a harness maker along Catsfield Stream but extended his business to include bicycles and motor bikes. He also operated a petrol pump. The shop was demolished *c.* 1970. (1909.)

UPFIELD'S WORKSHOP was further down the hill. Mr Upfield was originally a millwright and specialized in all aspects of agricultural engineering, but particularly in the repair of local windmills, before turning to motor engineering. By 1940 F.J. Parsons, the local printer, was using the premises, which were finally demolished in the 1960s. (1910.)

NORMANHURST COURT was built in the late 1860s by Thomas, Lord Brassey (the great railway engineer and traveller) in imitation of a French chateau. However, he never lived to see its completion. His son Thomas, the second Earl Brassey, (for 20 years Liberal MP for Hastings) inherited the house. During the First World War much of the house and grounds were converted into a military hospital, with Lady Idina as Commandant. Little physical evidence now remains of this magnificent building. Normanhurst suffered much damage in a fire on Sunday 2 August 1908, despite its reputation for being constructed with the latest fireproof technology. Unfortunately the delay in the arrival of fire tenders from Battle, Hastings and Bexhill allowed the fire to gain a strong foothold. It was finally demolished in 1951.

MUCH OF THE CONTENTS OF THE HOUSE was rescued as all the village men of Catsfield rushed to help. Here we see furniture, works of art and personal possessions piled on the lawn. The steam-powered fire engines can be seen working in the distance.

EARL BRASSEY HIMSELF inspects the fire damage at close quarters, coal scuttle in one hand and his other resting on a brass bedstead.

EARL BRASSEY decided that Normanhurst would, in future, need its own independent fire engine, manned by the estate's retainers, to avoid that critical delay. Here the estate's fire brigade poses in front of the Carriage House with its three new vehicles: the steam-powered fire engine, the extending ladder and, in the centre, the cart for the hose reel.

VOLUNTEERS FIELD DAY at Normanhurst, 24 July 1907. What a multiplicity of uniforms are on display here: local militia, sailors, marines (or naval landing parties) soldiers and members of the boys' brigade.

Robertsbridge and Salehurst

ROBERTSBRIDGE WOMEN'S INSTITUTE in fancy dress for a local fête in c. 1930: including Kate Taylor, Mrs Lusted, Mrs Hoad, Mrs Osman, Lily Bennett and Elsie Booth.

GEORGE HILL was the site of the fortnightly Cattle Auction and of the annual Fat Stock Show. The entrance to the market yard was to the left of the policeman in the distance. The market ceased to operate in the 1950s and much of George Hill is now built on. (1912.)

THE CHRISTMAS FAT STOCK SHOW was held annually on 12 December when local schools were closed for the day. The smartly dressed gentleman in the centre was J. Soan, in charge of the weight setting competition at the bullock pens. Organizing the Show in 1909 were F. Hudson and H. Bracewell.

ROBERTSBRIDGE HORSE SHOW was one of the highlights of the local rural calendar. It was traditionally held upon the Fair Field, now the Fair Meadow, while the accompanying pleasure fair was held close to the site of the new primary school. Here the carthorses are tethered for inspection in 1907.

IN THIS LATER PHOTOGRAPH of the Horse Fair (c. 1920), it has been transferred temporarily to the Recreation Ground, with the K & ES branch line embankment behind. The gelding carthorses are waiting to parade before the judges.

SOUTH END (*c.* 1910) before the construction of the War Memorial. The recently constructed brick building behind the wall on the right was sometimes used to garage the horse-drawn fire tender. The tile-hung house to the right of the Saddlery is now used as the Youth Centre.

POTATO PICKERS AT PARK FARM looking very elegant in their bonnets — or are the bonnets and aprons put on specially for the cameraman? Mrs Oliver, Mrs Harris, Mrs Milham and Mrs Willard fill their trugs.

THE EAST SUSSEX HUNT meet on the Green in front of The George in c. 1890. There really was a sizeable Green before the Hotel's car park, the Memorial's clock tower, the telegraph poles and the tree to commemorate Queen Victoria's 1897 Diamond Jubilee ate into it. Hilaire Belloc was impressed by the quality of the port wine at The George which served as the coaching inn for the village.

HIGH PAVEMENT used to be paved with red and blue bricks. Opposite, with Len Newbery's car outside, stood the premises of L.J. Nicholls, the cricket bats being manufactured in workshops at the back. He began making bats in 1876 and, in 1895, Dr W.G. Grace wrote him a letter of thanks for the bat with which he scored his 100th century and 1,000 runs in May. After several fires on the premises, the workshops were moved to Station Road.

THE WAR MEMORIAL has, here, only recently been constructed since it is not yet ivy-clad (1920). There is a lovely variety of vehicles on view: horse-drawn farm waggons, local delivery vans and a motor cycle and side-car.

MUCH OF THIS LOOKS VERY SIMILAR TODAY, except that now the tile-cladding has been stripped away to reveal the medieval frontages beneath. The projecting shop of J. Burchett was then a saddlery, hence the name of the antique shop now occupying the premises.

MR W.M. HILLS stands outside his High Street tobacconist and sweet shop, alongside his new delivery van. The shop has now reverted to a private dwelling, but the bus stop is still there.

THE WHITE HORSE with its fourteenth-century basement only recently ceased to operate as a pub. Robertsbridge Stores opposite, run by T. Hart, has now reverted to an attractive half-timbered property.

THE SEVEN STARS INN claims to be the oldest in the area, having been established in 1194. The original structure is a timber-framed Wealden house, with an open central hall with smaller apartments at either end, but it has been extensively altered over the centuries. The Congregationalists split with the local Methodists in 1876 and began meeting in a house on the High Street, which was then demolished for the erection of the brick church in 1881.

WATERS' STORES stocked the 'largest variety (of goods) in the district' claimed the advert printed on the reverse of this 1911 postcard. Not only does the shopfront claim he was a grocer and draper but clearly on display are: carpets, deckchairs, hardware, gardening equipment and the shop assistant even holds a can of Shell petrol.

LANGHAM TEMPERANCE HOTEL stood at the junction of Station Road on the site of the old Pig and Whistle Inn. There used to be a brewery run by the Robinsons at the rear, reached by a short passage off the High Street. In the 1920s the proprietors, Messrs Simes and Bashford, ran a teetotal hotel and set up a Tea Garden in the back garden. The corner section of the hotel is now a butcher's shop.

VEGETARIANS PLEASE AVERT YOUR EYES. What a magnificent Christmas display of meat c. 1910. Turkeys hide the name of W. Allen, 29 High Street, while the shop itself contains massive hides of beef, joints of lamb and pork, and even some lowly sausages. Presumably the pot plants were for garnishing!

TWO MEN repair the roof of Carter's shop, a draper's, at the north end of the High Street in c. 1910. I believe the man on the right to be the assistant of the photographer, Cooper, since he appears on several postcards of the area.

ROBERTSBRIDGE POST OFFICE. A posed study of the local postmen in c. 1900. It has since lost its weatherboarding and has reverted to its original half-timbering. Among those illustrated are Bert and George Markham and Sidney Beaney.

THE RAILWAY TAVERN on the left has long since been demolished and replaced by a garage and forecourt. It took its name from the arrival of the South Eastern Railway in 1851 and presumably catered for the needs of the navvies who were building the line.

THE LOWER END OF THE HIGH STREET (1904) showing the position of one of the three farriers who operated in Robertsbridge in 1900. The Smithy is the one-storey building on the right, with the posters on the wall, its entrance up the alleyway. Mr Hook, the blacksmith, lived in the adjoining house. Both properties now form the Meridien Restaurant.

THE JUNCTION WITH FAIR LANE C. 1910. The striped pole on the left signalled a barber's shop — a residue of the time when few people could read. The barber's, now a restaurant, even sold fishing tackle. The barber himself, a German, was interned during the First World War. The impressive looking Tudor House marks the position of the medieval George Inn.

JOHN WESLEY visited Robertsbridge on five occasions between 1771 and 1784. By 1812 a Methodist Chapel had been built in Fair Lane for the small number of adherents and this was enlarged in 1842. In 1874 a Sunday School was added. The chapel itself was converted into five flats in 1960.

FAIR LANE connected the Abbey with the village, deriving its name from the two-day annual fair held every September at Fairfield. It is the most picturesque part of Robertsbridge; since it never really developed into a through-road it has retained much of its old-world charm. The tile-hanging and weatherboarding of the cottages have now been stripped away, revealing beautiful half-timbered properties like Fayre Cottage.

MR AND MRS BARDEN sit on the steps of Tudor Rose cottage.

STATION ROAD is relatively modern, only being developed with the advent of the railway. The Working Men's Club & Institute was founded in 1892 but had to meet at the Langham Hotel until their clubhouse was opened in 1909 by Earl Brassey. On the right was Burgess' Corn Store, later converted into an ironmonger's. Note the pulley at roof level and the gas lamp outside the Institute, the only visible means of street lighting, c. 1910.

BOTH SHOPS ON STATION ROAD were run by Tom Croft, seen leaning on his fence. The shed with the corrugated roof sold bicycles which displayed a trademark featuring a design of Salehurst Church tower. The general store is now Bardens' the newsagents. Also illustrated are George Lusted, who worked in the cycle shop and Mabel Dick who organized the local newspaper deliveries.

STATION ROAD — clearly not yet tarmacked — has changed considerably since 1910. French's were still operating their undertaker's business in their wooden hut (out of the picture to the left) and had not yet built Brookside House. Sandcastle Cottages, visible through the trees, have now gone. Mr Burgess's Mill and Warehouse had not yet been built.

THE WAREHOUSE OF R. BURGESS & CO in Station Road, 1927. The firm specialized in foodstuffs for fattening and cramming poultry. The mill in which the grain was crushed and the maize 'kibbled' (i.e., coarsely ground) was directly behind the warehouse. The door on the left led to the shop which stocked all types of animal foods. The family firm was founded in 1848. The warehouse is now a garden machine centre. In the photograph are Mr Weeks and Dan Jones, who dressed the mill stones.

ROBERTSBRIDGE RAILWAY STATION was originally constructed by the SER in 1851, allowing passengers to reach London in 1½ hours instead of a two day coach journey. In this Victorian photograph, a four-horse-drawn waggonette, with two liveried postilions, collects a very elegantly dressed party of gentlefolk from the station forecourt. What social activity has brought so many worthies to the area I wonder?

THE NEW EXTENSION has now been added to the original William Tress design, to serve as a mess-room for the Kent and East Sussex crews who used Robertsbridge as their terminus, c. 1910.

A PANORAMIC VIEW of the platform at Robertsbridge c. 1910. On the far side of the gas-lit platform was the main line from Hastings to London. Passengers would have to disembark and cross over the line, on the now dismantled footbridge, to catch trains on the Kent and East Sussex branch line to Headcorn (built by the eccentric H.F. Stephens). Animals waiting for transportation would be kept in the cattle pens behind the white railings on the left. The station name was spelled out in whitewashed stones on the embankment. Beyond the station building can be seen the gantry and chimney (for the large steam boiler) of the timber yard where much of the machinery was steam-driven. It also powered a steam hooter which served the locality like a clock and was also used as the local air-raid siren.

RAILWAY STAFF pose on the platform at Robertsbridge c. 1905. Presumably the man with the bow tie and braided jacket is the Station Master. Most of the men wear caps clearly initialled 'SE & CR', but the boy on the left wears one bearing the branch line's initials 'K & ESR'.

THE LEVEL CROSSING GATES (c. 1908) on Station Road were operated by the gate keeper who lived in the adjoining house on the left, now demolished. The Ostrich Hotel, built c. 1855, relied heavily on its proximity to the station for its trade. In c. 1910 Charles Becker, a German, took over but he was interned at the beginning of hostilities and Charles Mabb became landlord.

HODSON'S MILL had the only private industrial siding on the K & ES branch line, with its own level crossing gates over the London road. The siding was first used in 1903 and the mill continued to operate freight on the line until 1969, several years after passengers ceased to be carried. In this photograph one of the bridges in the mill's grounds has collapsed beneath the weight of the two vans (Dec. 1928).

THE KENT & EAST SUSSEX BRANCH LINE operated from Robertsbridge to Tenterden and on to Headcorn, initially with the name Rother Valley Railway. Its operations began in 1900. Passenger carriage ceased on 2 January 1954, although some hop picker trains continued for a little longer; freight transportation was discontinued on 12 July 1961. Here two steam engines are being refilled from the water tower which stood just beyond where the line branched away from the main line (1961).

BRIGHTLING ROAD is the westerly extension of Station Road. This view, 100 yards west of the station, shows Woodland View which, in 1920, would have had beautiful rural views across the timber yard and the woodland around. In 1989 the view is obstructed by the construction of a large new housing development. Bungalows have also been built in most of the gaps along this stretch of road.

THIS PARTICULAR STRETCH OF LANGHAM ROAD has changed little in the past 50 years. The road surface remains unmade today. These houses were built in the mid-1930s after the sale of the Bugsell Estate in 1923 but the opposite roadside was only developed more recently. The field behind these houses used to be leased to the Air Council as the local airfield.

THE ENTRANCE TO DARVELL HALL on the junction of Brightling Road and Bishop's Lane which, until the last century, was the main road to Brightling (c. 1920).

IN LATER YEARS Darvell Hall, originally New House, became a well-known TB sanatorium, under the charge of Dr Dingley. Wooden huts were constructed with verandahs, allowing patient's beds to be brought out into the fresh air. Some huts were built on turntables so that the whole structure could be pushed around, depending on the direction of wind and sunshine. The Hall has more recently become the British centre for the Hutterian Bruderhof, a religious community of some 200 adherents.

A BEAUTIFUL ANIMATED STUDY of Northbridge Street in c. 1910. I assume the photographer must have knocked on all the doors to ask if the children could come out to add vitality to the scene.

NORTHBRIDGE STREET, looking north, showing the wooden carpenter's shop, long ago demolished. One of the village's three water pumps stood alongside it. (The other two were at Salehurst and Fair Lane). Keston Cottage's chimneys look rather different today.

APPARENTLY it was quite usual for schoolchildren to pop out at lunchtime to visit Mrs Harmer's shop in Northbridge Street, where they could queue up in winter to buy a cup of steaming cocoa costing ½*d*. (made with water) or 1*d*. (made with milk). The frontage of the shop itself, which projected into the roadway, was demolished for road widening.

NORTHBRIDGE STREET, looking southwards towards Robertsbridge, with Harmer's shop projecting into the roadway (1905).

THE LEVEL CROSSING at the Clappers marked where the K & ES branch line crossed the London road. It was operated by an old couple, Mr & Mrs Crowie Martin, who lived in one of the three cottages on the right (all now demolished). Whenever the area was flooded, they would live upstairs and clamber out of their window on a plank which led to the raised roadway!

ROADWORK being carried out at the Clappers in 1911, possibly connected with the strengthening of the bridge or the raising of the often flooded road surface. The Clappers is the name given to the series of bridges which span the Rother's flood plain.

ROBERTSBRIDGE FIRST AID HUT stood alongside the K & ES branch line at the bridge near the mill. On duty are S. Woodgate, H. French, C. Wilmer and G. Brooks. Behind can be seen the windmill which drove water from the River Rother to refill the steam trains.

ROBERTSBRIDGE FIRE BRIGADE pose at Mill Bay with their horse-drawn fire-tender. Apparently the horses were requisitioned whenever needed. It is tempting to assume that this may be the very engine and crew who fought the blaze at Hodson's Mill several years earlier.

HODSON'S MILL. A mill, originally called Ockham Mill, has stood on this riverbank site since the fourteenth century and would have serviced the milling needs of the whole community, with corn being carted in by the local farmers to be ground into flour. The two outside waterwheels of the timber watermill powered five pairs of mill stones. A corner of Mill House can just be seen, c. 1870.

A FIRE GUTTED THE MILL on 5 December 1902 causing massive structural damage. A collapsing masonry wall also fell onto Mill House. The fire raged for three days, the local volunteer fire brigade struggling to bring it under control with their hand-pumped hoses. Its new extension was fortunately undamaged and the mill itself was reconstructed with four storeys.

JAMES HODSON took over the mill in 1876 and two years later demolished ·it to build a massive five-storey brick edifice, certainly losing much of the rural charm of the earlier building. The horse-drawn covered waggons were no doubt a common sight throughout the neighbourhood as they made their deliveries, c. 1895.

HODSON'S STEAM TRACTION ENGINE, with its trailer, made deliveries throughout the locality; here at Eldridge's Stores at Westfield. George Pack, Percy Sands and Toby Standen pose in front of the vehicle.

THE FUNERAL OF MR HODSON, the mill owner, attracted mourners from the whole area. The photograph shows the moment when his coffin is being lifted from the hearse by the pall-bearers. Note the ceremonial guard of honour being formed by the local scouts and firemen.

THE NEW EIGHT BELLS, opposite the Salehurst junction, was completely renovated in 1905 and has since changed very little, except for the removal of the fencing. (The Old Eight Bells was the original name of the Salehurst Halt, one mile away). (1908.)

THERE HAD BEEN A 'SUBSCRIPTION SCHOOL' in Robertsbridge as early as 1796 where benefactors could donate one guinea and nominate a poor child from the parish to attend the school. In 1837 a plot of land was purchased from the nearby workhouse and a two-storey National School was built on the Salehurst junction (the upper storey for girls; the lower for the boys). The school now lies derelict. (c. 1910.)

CHURCH LANE JUNCTION, at the foot of Silver Hill, will never look the same again. Even the buildings which replaced the old garage have now been demolished for a new roundabout.

AN EDWARDIAN VIEW of the village of Salehurst, with Church Terrace on the left and the church tower rising majestically, looks much the same today. The village pump was set back from the road, where the white palings can be seen, just behind the girl.

THE COTTAGES OF POST OFFICE TERRACE — so called because the last property before the pub was the village post office, run by the Ganders. The pub, originally a thatched roadside inn, was still called the Old Eight Bells in 1912. The circular seat around the oak tree was melted down for munitions as part of the War Effort — along with most of the iron fences in Robertsbridge, e.g., those in the photograph of the Langham Hotel.

CHURCH BRIDGE was clearly two bridges until earlier this century. The wider cart bridge, now demolished, was used extensively by local farmers who drove their sheep and cattle to market over it. The footbridge to the left has since been rebuilt.

SALEHURST CHURCH'S BELLRINGERS pose for a photograph to commemorate ringing a peal of 5,040 changes on 28 October 1919. The board lists the team as: J. Goodsell, F. Morgan, J.H. Edwards, W.H. Hoad, T. Booth, T. Hoad, A.E. Edwards and E. Mills. It does not tell us how long the peal lasted nor how many parishioners applied for rate rebates.

WHAT A FINE GROUP OF MEN, almost certainly with a combined age of over 1,000 years. It is tempting to surmise that this group at Salehurst Church represent the 'Thirteen Ancient Men', the oldest men of the parish, together with the 'Three Just Men' they had to elect every three years to administer the Freeland's Charity which doled out free loaves of bread to the needy each Sunday.

OAST HOUSES AT PARSONAGE FARM, used to dry the hops which were – and still are – grown on the farm's hop-fields. Miss Elizabeth Hoad is seen feeding the chickens in 1920.

A SCENE, ALAS, TOO FAMILIAR TO US since the October 1987 hurricane. A large tree in the grounds of Salehurst Church caused extensive damage to the wall and outbuildings of Parsonage Farm, 1920. A horse-drawn reaper and binder stands on the left. A Second World War German bomb fell close to this spot, killing a horse and knocking over William Hoad.

HOP PICKERS' CELEBRATIONS AT ROBERTSBRIDGE c. 1870. Fancy dress festivities were traditionally held on the final day of hop-picking. Everyone (pickers, farm staff and children) would dress up and the women decorated their bonnets. Note the very unlikely looking policeman in the back row.

POLE PULLERS were part of the farm's staff and responsible for looking after a set of hop bins. They would cut down the bines, pull up the poles to allow their team of women to pick the hops and then load the hops onto the waggons for transporting to the oast house for drying. Posing with the pole-pullers is the measureman, c. 1870.

A FINE STUDY OF HOP PICKING in progress, probably at Glottenham Farm in 1914. Two women pick the hops into the bins (hessian bags supported on wooden frames) after the bines have been cut down from the supporting poles. A pile of stripped poles are in the background, while the bines to the left still await the pole pullers. The pickers were not paid by the hour but by the volume of hops picked. This was assessed by the measurer – here the farmer, William Hoad, waiting patiently with his wicker basket which served as a one-bushel measure. He would call out the number of bushels picked to the 'booker' (here his daughter Elizabeth), who would record the figure in her notebook. It took ten bushels to fill a poke, the large hop sack. Robertsbridge hop-farmers tended to use local labour, unlike in the larger hop-fields of Kent or even in the Guinness hop-fields at nearby Bodiam.

WALTER'S FARM, Poppinghole Lane, with farm workers and horses posing at the gate (1907). Farmer John K. Comber puffs at his pipe with son Steven on the horse. The oast houses survived until the October 1987 hurricane.

PARTS OF PARSONAGE FARMHOUSE date back to the fifteenth century, including the hall and beams. Shocks – or stooks – of oats are formed by six sheaves (loosely tied bundles) being placed upright alongside each other for mutual support, allowing the grain to dry and ripen.

THIS IDYLLIC RURAL SCENE (1906) shows a part of Robertsbridge which has long since disappeared. The Abbey pond has been filled in and the cottage has been demolished. Older inhabitants can still remember ice-skating on the frozen pond, the whole scene lit up by hurricane lamps hanging in the overhanging trees.

A HORSE-DRAWN MILK CART AT WALTER'S FARM in Poppinghole Lane c. 1910. On the cart, behind the 17 gallon milk churn, is Jim Pope. He was so shy he chose to marry a Miss Bishop at 8.00 a.m. to avoid the local crowds; so a Pope once married a Bishop at Salehurst Church.

MOWING. Here Steve Comber mows grass for hay with a side-mounted finger mower at Grove Farm, c. 1930. The 'tractor' is probably a converted car; such conversions being fairly common during the First World War and immediately afterwards. This field is now being bisected by the by-pass.

TURNING THE HAY. John K. Comber turns the hay for drying with a horse-drawn tedder at Walter's Farm, Poppinghole Lane, 1920.

RAKING THE HAY into long rows, the next part of the haymaking process. Mr Mills operates a horse-drawn hay rake at Walter's Farm in 1920.

CARTING THE HAY. A particularly beautiful study of a Sussex hay waggon; the hay supported by ash poles. Most of the workers carry long wide hay rakes, while the farmhand on the left has an unusual double-handled drag rake. A farmhand on the ground is using a long handled pitchfork to pass the hay up to the farmhand on top who only needs a short handled one. The carter, his trousers tied at the knees with yokes, carries a brass-bound whip. The farmer in his white coat is John Comber, while his son Steven is on top of the hay.

LOCAL RESEARCH is still needed on this posed study of woodworkers outside their Robertsbridge workshop c. 1880. With a cricket bat on view it would be very tempting to link this with Nicholls' workshop, but most of their tools are more identified with carpentry and joinery. The hut looks remarkably like French the undertaker's hut which used to stand on Station Road.

THE STAGE was built as a wooden lookout tower in 1900. It stood on top of Silver Hill, one of the highest points in Sussex, near where the Napoleonic Wars barracks had stood. Although popular with visitors who came to admire the views, it was never properly maintained and in 1934 it was declared unsafe for climbing. It was dismantled at the beginning of the Second World War.

THE ROBERTSBRIDGE ODD GANG. What a strange and intriguing caption to this posed photograph of a group of Robertsbridge's smartly dressed young men in *c.* 1910!

A RABBIT SHOOT AT DARWELL RESERVOIR in 1958 to cull the pre-myxomatosis rabbit population which was over-running parts of post-war rural Sussex. Local farmers join Harvey Harmer, the gamekeeper of the Egerton Estate, with a ferret box over his shoulder.

ROBERTSBRIDGE UNITED FC had a successful season in 1914 and their good fortune continued into the First World War, since none of their names appears on the Robertsbridge War Memorial. Back row: ? Routledge, G. Brooks, J. Neal, A. Carey, T. Duck, A. Turner, E. Jolley. Middle row: G. Willard, S. Severs, E. Gander. Front row: H. Duck, J. Duck, R. Jones.

ROBERTSBRIDGE CRICKET TEAM take the field at the Recreation Ground, c. 1928. I hope the players were loyal to local industry in their choice of bats (some made no doubt by Len Newbery himself). Left to right: W. Barnes, Len Newbery, -?-, S. Comber, W. Pankhurst, F. Fuller, A. Fuller and skipper Tom Barnes, the local grocer.

Mountfield, John's Cross and Vinehall

HOATHFIELD COTTAGES stand on the brow of Hoath Hill at Mountfield.

LOOKING UP HOATH HILL from Mountfield Stores. Riverhall was the name of the bridge at the foot of the hill.

MOUNTFIELD WORKHOUSE dates back to the time when parishes were expected to be responsible for their own poor and destitute. The New Poor Law of 1834 transferred this responsibility to Battle. Mountfield Workhouse stood on the junction of Hoath Hill, Church Lane and New Cut and has long been demolished. (1908.)

MOUNTFIELD POST OFFICE originally stood on the bend near the village pond, but was later moved into the general stores on Hoath Hill. The building has now reverted to a private dwelling called Church Cottage. (1910.)

MOUNTFIELD STORES stood at the bottom of Hoath Hill and acted as the village's general stores and post office until it was closed in 1987 and enterprisingly transformed into a pottery (c. 1910).

GYPSUM MINES. The mines were opened in 1875 by Messrs Bosworth, Ison and Pratt to extract gypsum (discovered while coal prospecting was in progress), a material used in a variety of products such as plasterboards, cement, pottery, plaster of Paris and chalk. The main shaft to the massive underground workings is 160ft deep. The above ground workings consist of kilns (where the gypsum is burnt) and crushing mills (where it is ground and bagged for transportation). The mine has its own railway line and sidings.

THE ABOVE GROUND WORKINGS which might be a potential eye-sore in this rural area are, in fact, very well masked from view by dense woodland, (only the aerial ropeway constructed in 1963 being visible in places). The coal-fired kilns were demolished in 1967.

PERMISSION WAS GIVEN for a turnpike road, a toll road, to be constructed from Watch Oak to John's Cross in 1836. Until then the main Battle – London road had run from Mount Street to Whatlington. This Victorian snapshot looks north along London Road towards the railway crossing, just beyond the figure in the roadway, c. 1890.

THE HAMLET OF JOHN'S CROSS lies along the London–Hastings road near the turn-off to Battle. Its weatherboarded sweet shop, with Mrs Selmes and her daughter at the gate, became a transport cafe but was gutted in a fire a few years ago and now lies derelict. The school can be seen in the distance. (1911.)

JOHN'S CROSS INN was built in 1511 as a thatched farm cottage and was converted to an ale-house in 1694. During the Napoleonic Wars it served as a local recruiting centre and was later used as a customs office and as a sorting office for the mail.

MOUNTFIELD SCHOOL, despite its name, lies outside the village on the John's Cross junction and also served the children of Whatlington. It was built in 1874. (1908.)

THE HAMLET OF VINEHALL STREET lies on the A21 between John's Cross and Whatlington. The ivy clad houses were built as part of the Vinehall Estate and stand opposite what used to be the village post office. (1908.)

THE BELL INN seen here in 1906, was built in the seventeenth century but closed as a public house in the early 1920s and was converted to a private dwelling, Bell Cottage. It continued to operate as the local working men's clubroom for several more years.

EVEN A SMALL HAMLET LIKE VINEHALL STREET used to warrant its own post office, built in 1890. It was run by the Whitings and also occupied by district nurse Dalloway. The speed of modern traffic along the A21 must have hindered business considerably and, by the late 1930s, it was closed and converted into two cottages. (1918.)

Whatlington

WOODMANS GREEN is the area immediately in front of the Royal Oak Inn. This part of the village is now dangerously bisected by the busy A21 but the photograph reveals a time when life was much quieter and less hectic. On the left is the old post office which also served as the village sweet shop (since demolished) in 1909.

J.H. POUND'S GENERAL STORE stood on the A21 near the Cripp's Corner junction. It later became the village post office. The speed and quantity of passing traffic and difficulties with parking must all have contributed to its closure for business in 1972. It has since been converted into a farmhouse. (1908.)

CHAPEL FORGE, (1910) with a trap outside awaiting the attention of T. Hyland the blacksmith, stopped operating in the mid-1950s and was demolished for the construction of a new house. The Wesleyan Chapel, closed as a church c. 1930, had been used as a reception centre for evacuees during the Second World War and has since been converted into a workshop and business.

THE ROYAL OAK was built *c.* 1490 and occupied what used to be an important junction when Whatlington Road served as the main London–Hastings road, before the New Road (the A21) was constructed. (1908.)

THE OLDEST PORTION OF LEEFORD FARMHOUSE was built in the fifteenth century as a hall house alongside the ford of the River Line. For many years there were hop gardens here (hence the oast house) but since 1982 an extensive vineyard has been developed. (1909.)

WHATLINGTON WATERMILL stood in the valley alongside Whatlington Road. By the early 1930s the wooden structure had become derelict and it was dismantled. On its site a topiary garden has been developed, attractively incorporating features of the stone foundations and the original water channels. (1908.)

THE MILL HOUSE opposite used to have a small building at the front which served as the mill's shop. During the war years Mill House was inhabited by Malcolm Muggeridge. (1908.)

Sedlescombe

THE HUNT meets on the Green in 1906. Behind can be seen the pillared shelter above the village pump, built in 1902. It was only in 1956 that a mains water system was supplied to Sedlescombe, at which point the well's water was declared unfit for human consumption.

A TURNPIKE ROAD was constructed from The Harrow (St Leonards) to Whatlington in the 1830s, to replace the zigzag of meandering country lanes which had complicated the route. This Victorian snapshot (c. 1890) is looking northwards from near the Marley Lane junction. The lady would now find herself standing dangerously in the middle of the A21, which follows the route of the toll road.

A GENERAL VIEW OF SEDLESCOMBE STREET from the south, looking across the fields and the River Brede, c. 1910.

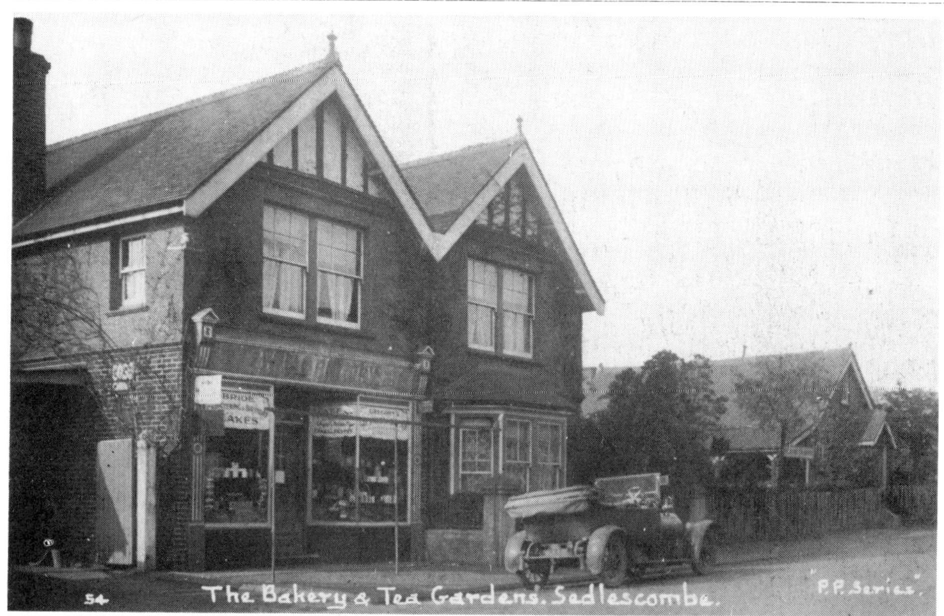

GREGORY'S BAKERY operated at the bottom of the village from the turn of the century. In its heyday up to 50 locals were employed within the bakery, shop or adjoining tea gardens.

WILLIAM BUTTON'S GROCERY AND DRAPERY STORE (1913) stood at the south end of the Green and, for a number of years until the 1920s, served as the village post office. On the far side of Barrack Cottage stood the Wesleyan Chapel, built c. 1815 but closed in 1924. During the war years it became a cinema and, more lately, an engineering workshop.

THE COACH AND HORSES used to be an attractive ivy clad pub c. 1910. Originally called The King's Head there has been an inn at the bottom of the Green since the eighteenth century.

WHILE MR FIELD THE LANDLORD went for a Sunday afternoon walk with his family on 15 February 1914, The Coach and Horses was gutted by fire, the flames no doubt fed by the ample supply of highly inflammable spirits on the premises. Much of the charm of the old structure was lost in the rebuilding.

THE QUEEN'S HEAD, built c. 1523, occupies a position at the top of the village green. The ivy clad and weatherboarded inn has a fine stagecoach parked outside, c. 1905.

CHURCH HILL joins Sedlescombe Street with the thirteenth-century parish church. There used to be three cottages on both sides of the hill, but they were all demolished in the 1930s. For a number of years this bungalow served as Sedlescombe's Infants' School, run by Miss Coggers and Miss Chiffany (c. 1910).

STREAM LANE runs from Sedlescombe Church, across the Brook, towards Whatlington and Battle, the New Road being constructed to meet it at Riccard's Lane. The farm on the left is Spilsteds, originally named Slaughters.

STREAM HOUSE, better known as Durhamford, is a beautiful early sixteenth-century timber-framed cross-winged yeoman's house, built alongside the bridge on Stream Lane. For almost a century, until the 1930s, it was divided into cottages but has now reverted to a single dwelling. (1910.)

Crowhurst

THE COTTAGES opposite the Recreation Ground show little sign of change in the last 80 years. (1910.)

THE PLOUGH INN, 1943. The message on the reverse of this postcard says: 'This was our village inn until Jerry paid it a visit last October. Three people were killed and several injured. They are patching it up to open again in Feb.'

THE AREA AROUND THE PLOUGH INN showing the devastation in October 1943 when a bomb exploded in the roadway. The blast severely damaged many buildings, including Mr Hutchinson's wheelwright's workshop opposite, and killed three people, including Mr and Mrs Hall. The Plough's name has been inked out in the photograph, presumably for censorship purposes.

A HUNT MEETING at The Plough, showing the wooden building on the left which was the local wheelwright's workshop, c. 1910.

THE SIGN ON THE DELIVERY CART (c. 1910) reads: 'R. West, coal & coke merchant & general carman, Crowhurst', probably at Croucher's Farm.

CROWHURST RAILWAY STATION C. 1910. The main line from Battle to Bo Peep Junction was opened by the SER on 1 February 1852, the final link connecting London with the coast, but a station was not constructed until the completion of the branch line in 1902.

THE CROWHURST–BEXHILL BRANCH LINE, only four miles long, was opened by the SE & CR on 1 June 1902 and closed in June 1964. Its outstanding feature was the massive viaduct with 17 arches, which crossed Crowhurst Marsh. The photograph shows a steam train near Adam's Farm, just north of the viaduct.

ADAM'S FARM, to the south of Crowhurst, c. 1910. The pond stood behind the palings on the right. The oast house was destroyed by a bomb from the same string which devastated the area around The Plough. A third bomb caused slight damage to the nearby railway viaduct, the presumed target.

AVONMOUTH TEA GARDENS was operated by the Goodsells who also ran a coal depot at the station yard. Tea was served in an old wooden rail carriage parked alongside what is now Cherry Tree House. In the foreground is a bridge over the stream.

CROWHURST POST OFFICE, now demolished, was run by the Wests and adjoined The Plough. It also served as the local general store, c. 1910.

IT WAS OBVIOUSLY A PROUD MOMENT for the village when the new telephone exchange was installed at the Post Office. Here Miss Marie West poses alongside the new equipment.

I WONDER WHAT FESTIVITIES have brought all the children of Crowhurst to the church with their flags and flowers – probably the 1911 Coronation celebrations. Behind them is the parish church of St George with its ancient yew tree, the oldest in Sussex. Legend states that William's Normans hanged a Saxon on the tree prior to the Battle of Hastings.

A VIEW FROM THE DAIRY BUILDINGS at Court Lodge Farm c. 1908. The unusual double oast house was demolished c. 1910 leaving two slight circular depressions in the pastureland. The house is Court Lodge with the ivy clad ruin of the old manor (built c. 1250 of Caen stone) behind.

ACKNOWLEDGEMENTS

I would like to express my gratitude to the following for the loan of photographs and assistance with my research:

E. & S. Harris • I. Doyle • F. Doyle • C. & J. Woodgate • J. & V. Barden
M. Salter • C.H. & J. C. Mabb • R.N.A. King • The George Inn (Robertsbridge)
H. Newbery • The Ash Tree Inn (Brownbread Street) • J. & L. Upton • P.E. &
V. Brett • P. Keeley • R. Syrett • A. Eves • G. Hilder • G. Wettle • K.J. Barnes
N. McNally • G. Munn • D. Hale • R. & L. Hart

BIBLIOGRAPHY

Battle Town & Country Guided Walk, Saxonwood WI.
Branch line to Tenterden, V. Mitchell & K. Smith (Middleton).
Bygone Battle, A. Guilmant (Phillimore).
Dallington Walk.
East Sussex Inns, B. Chapman (Countryside).
East Sussex Village Book, R. Taylor (Countryside).
History of Robertsbridge J.J. Piper (Belderson).
History of Salehurst, L.J. Hodson (L.J. Hodson).
Penny a Leg, F.A. Fisher.
Tonbridge to Hastings, V. Mitchell & K. Smith (Middleton).
Twenty Centuries in Sedlescombe, B. Lucey (Regency).
Victoria History of Counties of England: vol 9: Sussex, (OUP).
Victorian Sussex, J. Lowerson (BBC Radio Brighton).